BOOSTING
SELF-ESTEEM

A 4-week course to help Ch____
teenagers develop a positi____
self-image

by Nancy Going

Group®
Loveland, Colorado

Group®

Boosting Self-Esteem
Copyright © 1990 Group Publishing, Inc.

Credits
Edited by Stephen Parolini
Cover designed by Jill Bendykowski and DeWain Stoll
Interior designed by Jan Aufdemberge and Judy Atwood Bienick
Illustrations by Ed Koehler
Cover photo by David Priest and Brenda Rundback

ISBN 1-55945-100-9

17 16 15 14 13 12 11 10 9 8   03 02 01 00 99 98 97 96 95 94

Printed in the United States of America.

CONTENTS

BOOSTING SELF-ESTEEM

Marita's a beautiful, slightly overweight seventh-grader with long, dark hair and penetrating brown eyes. Her grades aren't great and she's into all kinds of rock music—just like all the boyfriends she tells you about. She's enthusiastic and energetic. But when it comes to participating in a group activity, you usually find her sitting by herself saying, "I can't do that!"

Barry's quiet and shy. His parents are going through a divorce. Barry can be difficult sometimes, especially when he and a couple of other guys disappear just when you're ready to get started. He usually does what you ask him to do in class, but he always clams up when it comes to sharing anything about himself.

Lawanda's always joking around and has a witty response for every question. You know she does pretty well in school. But she never takes anything seriously when she gets to church.

● ● ●

Girls	Guys
43%	24%

Percent of ninth-graders who agree with the statement: "Sometimes I think I'm no good."

How we feel about ourselves is at the root of much of our behavior. Self-esteem is an especially crucial issue for junior highers and middle schoolers. In a survey of over 90,000 teenagers by the Minnesota Department of Education, kids revealed their concern for how they feel about themselves.

In the same study, ninth-grade girls listed "Looks" as the #1 source of worry in their lives. Ninth-grade boys listed "Looks" as the third-highest worry, following "School" and "Having Friends."

In another study of fifth- to ninth-graders, 53 percent of young people said they worried very much or quite a bit about their looks. And 48 percent worried very much or quite a bit about how well other kids like them. Clearly, young teenagers struggle with self-esteem.

Kids who struggle with feeling good about themselves need encouragement. And the church can help provide that encouragement. When kids see their abilities as God-given gifts, they can feel good about who they are. When junior highers and middle schoolers recognize how God sees them, their self-esteem rises. And in a society where people place so much emphasis on physical looks, it's important for kids to base their self-esteem "not on what is seen, but on what is unseen. For what is seen is temporary, but what is unseen is eternal" (2 Corinthians 4:18b).

Boosting Self-Esteem will help your junior highers and middle schoolers see themselves as unique, worthwhile individuals. It'll help them give positive feedback to each other. And it'll help them feel good about who God made them to be.

HOW TO USE THIS COURSE

ACTIVE LEARNING

Think back on an important lesson you've learned in life. Did you learn it from reading about it? from hearing about it? from something you experienced? Chances are, the most important lessons you've learned came from something you experienced. That's what active learning is—learning by doing. And active learning is a key element in Group's Active Bible Curriculum.

Active learning leads students in doing things that help them understand important principles, messages and ideas. It's a discovery process that helps kids internalize what they learn.

Each lesson section in Group's Active Bible Curriculum plays an important part in active learning.

The **Opener** involves kids in the topic in fun and unusual ways.

The **Action and Reflection** includes an experience designed to evoke specific feelings in the students. This section also processes those feelings through "How did you feel?" questions and applies the message to situations kids face.

The **Bible Application** actively connects the topic with the Bible. It helps kids see how the Bible is relevant to the situations they face.

The **Commitment** helps students internalize the Bible's message and commit to make changes in their lives.

The **Closing** funnels the lesson's message into a time of creative reflection and prayer.

When you put all the sections together, you get a lesson that's fun to teach—and kids get messages they'll remember.

BEFORE THE 4-WEEK SESSION

● Read the Introduction, the Course Objectives and This Course at a Glance (p. 8).

● Decide how you'll publicize the course using the art on the Publicity Page (p. 9). Prepare fliers, newsletter articles and posters as needed.

● Look at the Bonus Ideas (p. 41) and decide which ones you'll use.

• Read the opening statements, Objectives and Bible Basis for the lesson. The Bible Basis shows how specific passages relate to junior highers today.

• Choose which Opener and Closing options to use. Each is appropriate for a different kind of group. The first option is often more active.

• Gather necessary supplies from This Lesson at a Glance.

• Read each section of the lesson. Adjust where necessary for your class size and meeting room.

• The approximate minutes listed give you an idea of how long each activity will take. Each lesson is designed to take 35 to 60 minutes. Shorten or lengthen activities as needed to fit your group.

• If you see you're going to have extra time, do an activity or two from the "If You Still Have Time . . ." box or from the Bonus Ideas (p. 41).

• Dive into the activities with the kids. Don't be a spectator. The lesson will be more successful and rewarding to both you and your students.

• The answers given after discussion questions are responses your students *might* give. They aren't the only answers or the "right" answers. If needed, use them to spark discussion. Kids won't always say what you wish they'd say. That's why some of the responses given are negative or controversial. If someone responds negatively, don't be shocked. Accept the person, and use the opportunity to explore other angles of the issue.

COURSE OBJECTIVES

By the end of this course your students will:
- learn what the Bible says about self-esteem;
- identify the difference between pleasing others and caring about others;
- receive positive feedback about their looks or abilities;
- evaluate how they feel about themselves and gain new perspective on how they feel about their looks;
- identify and affirm themselves as unique creatures created by God; and
- discover how caring for others increases self-esteem.

THIS COURSE AT A GLANCE

Before you dive into the lessons, familiarize yourself with each lesson aim. Then read the scripture passages.
- Study them as a background to the lessons.
- Use them as a basis for your personal devotions.
- Think about how they relate to kids' circumstances today.

LESSON 1: DO I LOOK OKAY TO YOU?
Lesson Aim: To help junior highers talk about and evaluate how they feel about their looks.
Bible Basis: 2 Corinthians 12:7-11 and Isaiah 52:13—53:3.

LESSON 2: AM I WHO OTHERS THINK I AM?
Lesson Aim: To help junior highers understand the difference between pleasing others and caring about others.
Bible Basis: Matthew 16:13-20 and Luke 7:36-50.

LESSON 3: MY ABILITIES
Lesson Aim: To help junior highers identify and affirm their unique God-given abilities.
Bible Basis: John 6:32-36; 8:12-16; 10:14-17; and 11:20-27.

LESSON 4: I CAN MAKE A DIFFERENCE
Lesson Aim: To help build self-confidence in junior highers.
Bible Basis: Genesis 17:1-8 and Matthew 16:13-19.

PUBLICITY PAGE

Grab your junior highers' attention! Copy this page, then cut and paste the art of your choice in your church bulletin or newsletter to advertise this course on self-esteem. Or copy and use the ready-made flier as a bulletin insert.

Splash this art on posters, fliers or even post-cards! Just add the vital details: the date and time the course begins, and where you'll meet.

It's that simple.

BOOSTING SELF-ESTEEM

A 4-week junior high course on self-esteem

Come to _____

On _____

At _____

Come learn how to feel good about your God-given abilities.

DO I LOOK OKAY TO YOU?

Personal appearance is a big source of worry for many junior highers and middle schoolers. It's hard for them to feel good about the gifts God's given them when they focus on their physical imperfections.

To help junior highers talk about and evaluate how they feel about their looks.

LESSON AIM

Students will:
● discuss how people feel about their looks;
● study how God uses people's limitations;
● evaluate how much they worry about their looks; and
● receive positive feedback about their looks or abilities.

OBJECTIVES

Look up the following scriptures. Then read the background paragraphs to see how the passages relate to your junior highers or middle schoolers.

In **2 Corinthians 12:7-11**, Paul tells about his physical limitations.

Scholars have suggested several possibilities for what Paul refers to as the "thorn in my flesh." Some believe Paul may have been referring to migraine headaches, eye trouble, malaria or even epilepsy. Whatever the "thorn" really was, it helped him remain humble. He was aware he was God's instrument and didn't need to be perfect to do God's work.

Junior highers have a hard time accepting their perceived inadequacies. But like Paul, they can realize they're still God's instruments.

In **Isaiah 52:13—53:3**, Isaiah begins to describe the "suffering servant."

This passage describes the suffering servant—Jesus—as a man of ordinary appearance and lowly background. Yet Isaiah

BIBLE BASIS
2 CORINTHIANS 12:7-11
ISAIAH 52:13—53:3

also describes the suffering servant as being greatly exalted.

Junior highers who feel they aren't worth much can look to this description of Jesus for assurance that they, too, can do God's work no matter how "ordinary" they are.

THIS LESSON AT A GLANCE

Section	Minutes	What Students Will Do	Supplies
Opener (Option 1)	5 to 10	**Picture Perfect**—Create pictures of people with "perfect" features.	Paper, pencils, magazines, tape
(Option 2)		**Wish List**—Determine one physical feature they'd like to have.	Paper, pencils
Action and Reflection	10 to 15	**Adult Survey**—Survey adults on how they feel about appearance.	Copies of "Survey Questions" box, (p. 13), pencils, paper
Bible Application	10 to 15	**God Uses Limitations**—Learn how God can work through people's limitations.	Bibles, newsprint, markers
Commitment	10 to 15	**Do I Look Okay?**—Reflect on how much they worry about looks.	"Do I Look Okay?" handouts (p. 17), pencils, markers, newsprint
Closing (Option 1)	up to 5	**Good Features**—Tell a partner what they appreciate about his or her appearance.	Magazines, Bibles
(Option 2)		**What I Have**—Thank God for positive features or talents they have.	

The Lesson

OPENER
(5 to 10 minutes)

OPTION 1: PICTURE PERFECT

Form pairs. Distribute paper, pencils and several copies of a teen magazine to each pair. Ask partners each to look through the pictures in the magazines and make up a wish-list of physical features they wish they had. Then have teenagers each tear the pictures out of the magazines and tape them to paper to create a composite of the "perfect person." Have partners discuss their creations.

Form a circle. Have kids display their creations.

Ask:

● **What do you notice about the composite creations?** (They're all "perfect"; they look pretty silly.)

● **Are people generally happy or unhappy about the way they look? Explain.** (Unhappy, they always feel there's something that's not right; happy, most people like how they look.)

Say: **Appearance is important to many people. It's often easier to criticize our appearance than praise it. Today we'll look at how we view ourselves and how God sees us.**

OPTION 2: WISH LIST

Give teenagers each a piece of paper and a pencil. Have them each write down one famous person's physical feature they'd like to have. For example, someone might want a famous athlete's biceps or a singing star's nose. Tell kids you'll be reading the papers aloud. Collect the papers and read the features people wrote. Then form a circle.

Ask:

● **Why do people admire physical attributes of famous people?** (They wish they looked like the famous people; they like the way they look.)

● **Do most people feel good about the way they look? Why or why not?** (Yes, they like at least one thing about the way they look; no, they wish they could be perfect.)

Say: **We're going to find out just how important our looks are. We'll begin by finding out how adults feel about their looks.**

ADULT SURVEY

Arrange ahead of time with an adult Sunday school class to have kids spend no more than six minutes surveying the adults. If you're meeting at a time when no adult classes are meeting, have teenagers do a quick phone survey of at least one adult each during the class. Or arrange ahead of time to have teenagers survey parents or other adults before the class.

Copy the "Survey Questions" from the margin and have kids each ask an adult the questions and record his or her answers on a piece of paper.

Have kids thank the adults for their participation in the survey. When the students return, have them share the results with the entire group.

Ask:

● **What surprised you most about what the adults said? Explain.**

● **How do you think movie stars, rock stars and other famous people might answer the question: "How important are looks?"** (They'd say looks are very important; they'd say they aren't important, it's talent that's important.)

Have teenagers each name one famous person they think is especially good-looking. Have the rest of the teenagers re-

---

ACTION AND REFLECTION
(10 to 15 minutes)

Survey Questions

● What one physical feature of yours do you like least? Why?

● What's your best physical feature?

● How important are looks: very important, somewhat important or not very important at all? Explain.

spond to each person's choice with applause if they agree or booing if they disagree.

Ask:

● **Did everyone agree with each person's choice of a good-looking person? Why or why not?** (No, each person likes different things about appearance; mostly, there are people who everyone likes.)

Say: **Not only junior highers think about their appearance. Adults have the same concerns. Even famous people are concerned about how they look. But we found that each of us has a different definition of what's good-looking. Next, we'll gain a unique perspective on looks from the Bible.**

BIBLE APPLICATION
(10 to 15 minutes)

GOD USES LIMITATIONS

Have the students form groups of no more than four. Ask each group to look up the following scripture passages and talk about what the passages say about how we feel about looks: 2 Corinthians 4:15-18; 12:7-11; and Isaiah 52:13—53:3.

Give groups each a sheet of newsprint and a marker. Have groups each make a list of physical inadequacies people have. Ask kids to be general and not name names. For example, someone might list crooked nose, pimples or big ears. Then have them each make another list—based on the scripture passages—that describes how God uses people no matter what their appearance. For example, someone might list God's power is perfected in weakness or the suffering servant will prosper. Have groups tell about their lists.

Ask:

● **How do you feel about the description of the suffering servant in Isaiah 52:13—53:3?** (I feel sorry for him; it bothers me.)

● **If God uses people who aren't physically perfect, what does that say about the importance of good looks?** (Good looks don't determine your worth; God isn't interested in physical appearance.)

● **Does that mean appearance isn't important at all? Explain.** (No, it's still important to take care of your body; yes, physical appearance doesn't matter at all—it's what's inside that counts.)

Say: **According to 2 Corinthians 4:18, things that are seen are temporary and things that are unseen are eternal.**

Ask:

● **What unseen things do you think Paul was talking about in this passage?** Have kids look up 1 Corinthians 13 for answers to this question. (Love; hope; concern for others.)

Say: **The key to feeling good about how we look is to use *God's* standard of good looks rather than our own. But sometimes, it's not easy to see ourselves the way God sees us.**

DO I LOOK OKAY?

Give students each a copy of the "Do I Look Okay?" handout (p. 17) and a pencil. Tell kids they won't have to share their answers with anyone. Have them each complete the handout and score the results using the guide at the bottom.

Have kids spend a moment or two in silence meditating on the results of their handouts. Remind kids this is a time to think seriously about how they feel about the importance of looks.

Then form a circle. Have kids brainstorm practical ways to refocus how they feel about appearance if they place too much importance on it. For example, have people brainstorm ways they can use their abilities to help others, such as helping someone with homework, babysitting for a friend or teaching a friend a song. Write these suggestions on a sheet of newsprint. Have junior highers each initial one idea on the list and commit to try this idea.

OPTION 1: GOOD FEATURES

Say: **While we may or may not be beautiful enough to be on the cover of Seventeen magazine or star in the latest teen movie, God gave each of us beautiful features we can be happy about.**

Have students each choose a partner, preferably someone they feel comfortable with. Spread around magazines on the floor. Have kids each tear from a magazine a picture of a physical feature that represents something they like about their partner's appearance. Have kids each present the picture to their partner and tell why they chose it. For example, someone might tear out a picture of eyes and say "I chose eyes because God gave you beautiful eyes." Be sensitive to kids who may feel uncomfortable with this activity, and remind kids to be sincere.

Close by reading aloud Psalm 139:13-16 in unison.

OPTION 2: WHAT I HAVE

Form a circle. Have kids each think of one physical feature they desire but don't have, and one feature or talent they do have. Then go around the circle and have teenagers each tell both using the following format: "I may not have (desired feature), but I thank God for (feature or talent they do have)." After each person speaks, have the rest of the group say in unison, "Thank you, Lord, for making us who we are."

Then close with prayer, thanking God for each student. Be specific in your prayer, and identify one feature or talent you appreciate about each junior higher.

COMMITMENT
(10 to 15 minutes)

CLOSING
(up to 5 minutes)

If You Still Have Time . . .

Body Collage—Form groups of no more than six. Distribute magazines and tape. Have groups each tear out pictures to make a collage of body parts that can be used to serve God. Have them identify how the body parts can be used to serve God. For example, someone might say the eyes can see others in need or the mouth can tell others about God's love. Have groups each share their completed collages.

"God Loves You as You Are" Cards—Have the kids each choose one adult from the Adult Survey in the Action and Reflection section and make a "God loves you as you are" card for that person. Have kids also thank the adults for their participation in the survey.

DO I LOOK OKAY?

This handout will help you think about how much value you place on your looks. Answer the questions honestly. Check "often," "sometimes" or "never" for each item. Then score yourself according to the instructions at the bottom.

	Often	Sometimes	Never
1. I compare my looks to my friends.	☐	☐	☐
2. I'm proud of things I've done.	☐	☐	☐
3. I worry about how I look.	☐	☐	☐
4. I think I'm attractive.	☐	☐	☐
5. I see people who're more attractive than me and it bothers me.	☐	☐	☐
6. I think God did a good job creating me in his image.	☐	☐	☐
7. I wish I could change things about the way I look.	☐	☐	☐
8. I feel good about my abilities and talents.	☐	☐	☐
9. I'm afraid to try out for plays or musicals because I don't look good enough.	☐	☐	☐
10. I can accept how I look.	☐	☐	☐
11. I get embarrassed if I'm around people who I think are ugly.	☐	☐	☐
12. I get along with people who look different from me.	☐	☐	☐

SCORING: For each question you answered "sometimes," give yourself one point. For each odd-numbered question you answered "often," give yourself two points (no points for "never"). For each even-numbered question you answered "never," give yourself two points (no points for "often").

0 to 8 points	Good job! You keep your looks in focus. Celebrate your balanced approach to looks by encouraging someone else in the class.
9 to 18 points	You're a bit out of focus. Although you probably aren't unhappy, you can still improve how you feel about your looks.
19 to 24 points	You tend to worry about how you look. Learn to accept and celebrate the abilities and talents God's given you. Talk to a friend about how to refocus how you feel about your looks.

LESSON 2

AM I WHO OTHERS THINK I AM?

Junior highers often feel bad when they don't live up to others' expectations. And sometimes, others' expectations may shape how junior highers act. Junior highers may begin to please others in order to feel accepted. Then their self-esteem hinges on how others see them.

LESSON AIM

To help junior highers understand the difference between pleasing others and caring about others.

OBJECTIVES

Students will:
- discover how to be themselves and care about others;
- discover how Jesus dealt with people's expectations;
- identify things they do to please others; and
- tell why they appreciate each other.

BIBLE BASIS

MATTHEW 16:13-20
LUKE 7:36-50

Look up the following scriptures. Then read the background paragraphs to see how the passages relate to your junior highers or middle schoolers.

In **Matthew 16:13-20**, Jesus asks Peter what others are saying about him.

Throughout his ministry, Jesus met people who felt he didn't live up to their expectations of him. But he did live up to God's expectations.

It's important for junior highers to see not only that Jesus dealt with this issue, but also how he taught others to deal with it. Just as Jesus knew he had to live up to his father's expectations first, junior highers need to learn to identify whose expectations are most important to live up to.

In **Luke 7:36-50**, a woman who's a sinner anoints Jesus with perfume.

Jesus spent a lot of time with people who didn't live up to others' expectations. The Pharisees—and even his own disciples—couldn't understand why Jesus didn't send these people away. Jesus accepted anyone who had faith in him.

Jesus' acceptance is important for junior highers who feel they can't live up to others' expectations. Jesus accepts them as they are—even if other people see them as inferior.

THIS LESSON AT A GLANCE

Section	Minutes	What Students Will Do	Supplies
Opener (Option 1)	5 to 10	**Picture This**—Describe each other.	Instant-print camera, tape, paper, pencils
(Option 2)		**Your Favorite Things**—Guess each other's favorite things.	
Action and Reflection	10 to 15	**Expectations for Me**—Mime actions illustrating how others see them.	
Bible Application	10 to 15	**Caring and Pleasing**—Learn how Jesus dealt with pleasing others.	Bibles, copies of "Caring Questions" box (p. 21)
Commitment	5 to 10	**Clearer Pictures**—Evaluate what they do for others and for themselves.	"Clearer Pictures" hand-outs (p. 24), pencils
Closing (Option 1)	up to 5	**From the Heart**—Tell why they care about each other.	Paper, markers
(Option 2)		**I Care**—Share reasons they care about each other.	

The Lesson

OPTION 1: PICTURE THIS

Take an instant-print picture of each student. Mix up the pictures, and pass them out. Have the students each tape the picture they received to a piece of paper. Have students each write seven words or phrases on the paper to describe that person in a positive way. For example, someone might write "likes music" or "gets good grades." Remind kids to be sincere. If someone doesn't know the person in the picture, en-

OPENER
(5 to 10 minutes)

courage that person to guess about him or her on the basis of the picture.

Say: **People assume things about you by how you look or act. At times, what they expect and who you really are may be very different.**

Have kids give the pictures back to their original owners. Then have each teenager explain how much of what was written is true and how much is false.

Say: **Often others' expectations shape how we act or what we say. Today we're going to study the difference between trying to meet others' expectations and learning to care about others.**

OPTION 2: YOUR FAVORITE THINGS

Form a circle, and have one junior higher stand in the center of the circle. If you have a large class, form circles of six to eight kids each. Have teenagers guess the following things about the person in the circle:

- What's this person's favorite color?
- What's this person's favorite free-time activity?
- What's this person's favorite class in school?
- What's this person's favorite food?

After teenagers guess the answers for the person in the center of the circle, have the person tell how he or she would honestly answer the questions. Repeat the activity until all kids have had a chance in the center of the circle.

Ask:

- **Was it easy to guess the right answers for every person? Explain.** (Yes, I know these kids well; no, I don't know everyone that well.)
- **Why are people's perceptions of others often inaccurate?** (Because they don't really know the people; because people don't see the real person.)

Say: **How others perceive us can affect how we act. If someone expects us to be loud, it's probably easy to be loud. Sometimes we begin to focus on meeting others' expectations instead of simply caring about others. Today we'll look at how we can care about others—but still be ourselves.**

EXPECTATIONS FOR ME

Form groups of no more than four. Have groups each stand and form a circle, facing inward. Then have them each mime an activity that fits the following categories:

- The image my friends have of me is . . .
- The image my parents have of me is . . .
- The image I have of myself is . . .

Encourage kids to use facial expressions and motions to illustrate the images. Then have kids discuss their actions briefly in their groups.

ACTION AND REFLECTION

(10 to 15 minutes)

Ask:

● **Was there a difference in your actions from one category to the next? Explain.** (Yes, my parents and friends have different images of me; no, I am just what everyone sees.)

● **How did you feel about acting differently for each category?** (Embarrassed; confused; uncomfortable.)

● **Do others' expectations of how you should act affect how you act? Explain.** (Yes, sometimes I act different so people will accept me; no, I don't let others' expectations affect me.)

Say: **When we act according to others' expectations, it's often because we want to please them or be accepted. But when we seek to please others, it sometimes keeps us from being ourselves. Instead of striving to please others, we should learn to be ourselves and care for others.**

CARING AND PLEASING

Say: **Jesus dealt with the issue of how to please others. He also dealt with others' expectations.**

Form groups of no more than four. Have each group read Matthew 16:13-20 and Luke 7:36-50. Give each group a copy of the "Caring Questions" box in the margin. Have groups each discuss the questions based on the passages.

Have groups each brainstorm two or three differences between pleasing someone and caring about someone. Have them report these differences to the other groups.

Say: **Jesus knew his mission was different from what many people thought it should be. But he didn't change his ways to please others. Instead, he used who he was to care about others.**

BIBLE APPLICATION
(10 to 15 minutes)

Caring Questions

● Who did people think Jesus was?

● How do you feel when people describe you as being like someone else?

● Did Jesus change his actions to meet others' expectations? Why or why not?

● Did Jesus try to please others or care for them? Explain.

● How did Jesus care for people in these passages?

Table Talk

The Table Talk activity in this course helps junior highers and middle schoolers discuss self-esteem with their parents.

If you choose to use the Table Talk activity, this is a good time to show students the "Table Talk" handout (p. 25). Ask them to spend time with their parents completing it.

Before kids leave, give them each the "Table Talk" handout to take home, or tell them you'll be sending it to their parents.

Or use the Table Talk idea found in the Bonus Ideas (p. 42) for a meeting based on the handout.

COMMITMENT
(10 to 15 minutes)

CLEARER PICTURES

Give each student a copy of the "Clearer Pictures" handout (p. 24) and a pencil. Ask kids each to follow the instructions and complete their handout. Explain that they won't have to share all their answers.

Form pairs. Have partners each tell how they completed the handout—if comfortable doing so.

Ask them to discuss the following questions:

● **How does this handout give you a clearer picture of who you are?**

● **How do you feel about the items you marked "Because I Want To"?**

● **How do you feel about the items you marked "Because Others Expect Me To"?**

● **Based on your answers, do you do things out of sincerity or because of others' expectations?**

Say: **God wants us to be who we are and to develop as individuals. He wants us to care about others because we want to—not because we feel we have to.**

Have kids each silently complete the following sentence after you read it aloud: **One way I can strive to be who God wants me to be is . . .**

CLOSING
(up to 5 minutes)

OPTION 1: FROM THE HEART

Give kids each a piece of paper and a marker. Have them each quickly tear the paper into the shape of a heart. Then have kids form a circle.

Say: **When we do things because others expect us to, we may be untrue to ourselves. Instead, God wants us to do things from the heart.**

Have kids each write on their paper heart why they care for the person on their right. Remind them to be sincere. Then have them each present their heart to the appropriate person.

Close by reading aloud: **"For we are God's workmanship, created in Christ Jesus to do good works, which God prepared in advance for us to do"** (Ephesians 2:10).

OPTION 2: I CARE

Say: **Just as Jesus didn't compromise who he was in order to simply please others, we need to avoid compromising who we are. We need to show people we truly care about them.**

Have kids tell each other why they care about one another using the following procedure. Form pairs. Have partners take turns completing the sentence: "I care about you because . . ." Then form a circle. Tell students why you care about them. Be specific. Close with silent prayer.

Before Next Week's Lesson—If you plan to use the Baby Bonanza Opener in the next lesson, tell kids to each bring in a baby picture from home. Or collect baby pictures from parents prior to the class. If you have a small class, you might want to bring in baby pictures of other familiar congregation members. Have at least five pictures available for this activity.

If You Still Have Time . . .

Masks—Have students describe "masks" people wear when they try to please others. Then have kids discuss how they feel when they put on masks or see people who put on masks. For fun, have kids each make a mask out of paper bags or paper plates representing one of these false fronts.

Who God Wants—Form groups of no more than four. Have groups each come up with a poem or rap song describing who God wants them to be.

pg 21
24
25
red or pink paper

CLEARER PICTURES

For each item, place a mark in the column that best describes why you do it.

	Because I Want To	Because Others Expect Me To	Doesn't Apply
1. I try to get good grades.			
2. I try to be funny.			
3. I do things to make people happy.			
4. I help others.			
5. I follow the rules.			
6. I strive to be good at sports.			
7. I try to be popular.			
8. I do what my friends are doing.			
9. I like certain kinds of music.			
10. I make money.			
11. I have a boyfriend or girlfriend.			
12. I help friends with homework.			
13. I read my Bible.			
14. I go to church.			
15. I spend time praying.			

Table Talk

To the Parent: This month, we're talking about self-esteem at church. Please take time to sit down with your junior higher or middle schooler and discuss this issue together.

Parent (Complete the following sentences.)
- When I was a young teenager, my self-image was . . .
- When friends wanted me to be someone I wasn't, I responded by . . .
- As an adult, I struggle with feeling good about myself when . . .

Junior higher (Complete the following sentences.)
- The way I feel about myself is . . .
- When my friends expect me to be someone I'm not, I respond by . . .
- I struggle with feeling good about myself when . . .

Parent and junior higher
- Tell each other one thing you dislike about the way you look.
- Tell each other one thing you like about the way you look.
- Share at least two ways you can help each other build self-esteem.
- Tell about a time when you had little or no self-confidence. Discuss how you felt and how you got through that time.
- Say at least three things you appreciate about each other.
- Read Genesis 1:26-27 together. Discuss what it means to be made in God's image.
- Complete the following sentence: God sees me as a person who . . .

During the coming week, surprise each other by doing something for each other without being asked. You might bake cookies, buy dinner, make a present or write a poem. Think of a creative way to show you care for each other.

Close by praying together, asking God to help you become the people he created you to be.

LESSON 3

MY ABILITIES

Sometimes it's easier for junior highers to see others' strengths and abilities than their own. When they don't see their own abilities, they may feel inferior or even worthless. But junior highers can build their self-esteem when they learn to recognize their own unique qualities.

LESSON AIM

To help junior highers identify and affirm their unique God-given abilities.

OBJECTIVES

Students will:
● discover how each person has different abilities and gifts;
● see how Jesus understood his uniqueness and abilities;
● determine their unique abilities; and
● celebrate each other's uniqueness.

BIBLE BASIS

JOHN 6:32-36
JOHN 8:12-16
JOHN 10:14-17
JOHN 11:20-27

Look up the following scriptures. Then read the background paragraphs to see how the passages relate to your junior highers or middle schoolers.

In **John 6:32-36; 8:12-16; 10:14-17;** and **11:20-27**, Jesus describes himself with "I am" statements.

In each of these short passages, Jesus reveals something about himself. He describes himself as the bread of life, the light of the world, the good shepherd, and the resurrection and the life. Each phrase sheds light on both the nature of Jesus and his mission on Earth. Jesus knew who he was and how important it was to be connected with God's will.

Junior highers struggle to know who they are. By examining Jesus' life, they can be challenged to do God's will as they learn about who they are.

Section	Minutes	What Students Will Do	Supplies
Opener (Option 1)	5 to 10	**Baby Bonanza**—Identify their unique qualities in baby pictures.	Baby pictures, tape, paper, pencils, cookies
(Option 2)		**Creation Celebration**—Create collages of things God created.	Magazines, tape
Action and Reflection	15 to 20	**Unique People Hunt**—Search for people with unique characteristics.	"Unique People" hand-outs (p. 32), pencils
Bible Application	5 to 10	**I Am**—Discuss Jesus' uniqueness and how he used his abilities.	Bibles, newsprint, markers
Commitment	10 to 15	**This Is Me**—Identify and reflect on their unique abilities.	"This Is Me" handouts (p. 33), pencils
Closing (Option 1)	up to 5	**Unique Creation**—Affirm each other as God's creation.	Paper, tape
(Option 2)		**Talents**—Identify talents and abilities in each person.	

The Lesson

OPTION 1: BABY BONANZA

OPENER
(5 to 10 minutes)

Before the Lesson—Have kids each bring in a baby picture from home, or collect them from parents prior to the class. If you have a small class, you might want to bring in baby pictures of other familiar congregation members. Have at least five pictures available for this activity.

Carefully tape the baby pictures to a wall. Under each picture, tape a piece of paper with a number on it. Have kids each write on a blank piece of paper the numbers from the pictures. Then give them a few minutes to look over the pictures and silently guess who's who and write their guesses next to the appropriate numbers on their papers. Tell kids not to help each other.

When everyone's done, go through the pictures and have kids tell who they think is in each picture. After correct guesses are made, ask what unique feature helped make an accurate guess. Have kids each count their correct guesses and award a box of cookies to the person with the most correct guesses. Or have multiple winners share the box of cookies.

Ask:

● **What features made it easy to guess some of the pictures?** (Eye color; head shape; dimples.)

Say: **Just as each of the babies in these pictures has unique features, so each of us has unique abilities and gifts. But finding these gifts is sometimes as hard as identifying the right person in these baby pictures. Today we're going to examine what our gifts are and how we can use them.**

OPTION 2: CREATION CELEBRATION

Place magazines and tape on the floor. Be sure to include nature magazines as well as magazines with people in them. Designate a wall in the room to be a "mural wall." Have kids silently tear out pictures and words representing God's creation and tape them to the mural wall.

After a few minutes, have kids form a semicircle facing the wall.

Ask:

● **Are there any major elements missing from this mural? Explain.**

● **Which picture best represents God's creation to you? Explain.** (Nature pictures, because I like nature; pictures of people, because God created people in his image.)

● **How do you celebrate God's creation?** (I go on walks; I like hiking; I enjoy being outside; I enjoy talking with friends.)

● **Based on the pictures on the wall, does everyone enjoy the same parts of God's creation? Explain.** (No, some people like nature rather than people; no, some people don't like babies or pictures of people.)

Say: **God created a varied and interesting world around us. And he also created a variety of people to inhabit the world. Today we're going to discover how each of our unique interests and abilities is a gift from God.**

Table Talk Follow-Up

If you sent the "Table Talk" handout (p. 25) to parents last week, discuss students' reactions to the activity. Ask volunteers to share what they learned from the discussion with their parents.

UNIQUE PEOPLE HUNT

Form pairs. Give each pair a copy of the "Unique People" handout (p. 32). Tell pairs they will each go around the room and into other classrooms (arrange this ahead of time) to find people who can perform the activities or admit to the statements. Tell kids each person may sign no more than two lines. Set a 10-minute time limit for pairs to collect as many signatures as possible and return to the classroom. After the time is up, have pairs each share their handout with the other kids.

Form a circle.

Ask:

● **How did you feel when you tried to collect the signatures?** (Embarrassed; impatient; uncomfortable.)

● **Were you surprised how many different talents and unique qualities were displayed by the people in this class (and other classes)? Why or why not?** (Yes, I never thought I'd get this many signatures; no, I knew we had strange people in this class.)

● **How are these strange or unique qualities like the differences in each person here in this room?** (We all have different abilities or skills; some people do some things better than others.)

Have kids each call out abilities or talents they see in people around them. Keep things moving.

Then ask:

● **Is it always easy to know what your abilities are? Explain.** (No, I sometimes think I don't have any special abilities; yes, I know what I can and can't do.)

Say: **There are two steps to becoming the best person you can be. The first is identifying your unique abilities and gifts. The second is using those abilities and gifts. Next we'll take a look at how Jesus used his gifts.**

I AM

Form groups of no more than four. Assign each group one of the following scriptures: John 6:32-36; John 8:12-16; John 10:14-17; and John 11:20-27. Give each group a sheet of newsprint and a marker. Have groups each make a picture or symbol that describes who Jesus says he is or how he used his abilities. Then have groups each share and discuss their picture with the whole group.

Ask:

● **How did Jesus describe himself?**

● **How did he use his gifts and abilities to do God's will?** (He cared for people; he taught people; he healed people.)

Say: **Jesus was confident about who he was because he knew his abilities and how to use them. Knowing our own abilities can help build our confidence. But how well do you know your abilities? Next we'll take a look at how well we know ourselves and how well others know us.**

ACTION AND REFLECTION
(15 to 20 minutes)

BIBLE APPLICATION
(5 to 10 minutes)

John 6:32-36
8:12-16
14-17
10:
11 – 20-27

COMMITMENT
(10 to 15 minutes)

THIS IS ME

Form pairs. Distribute the "This Is Me" handout (p. 33) and pencils. Have partners follow the instructions on the handout.

Form a circle.

Ask:

● **Did you learn anything new about yourself? Explain.** (Yes, I learned I had abilities I didn't think I had.)

Have kids share one or two of their abilities with the whole group. For each one shared, ask:

● **How can this ability be used to help others? to further God's kingdom?**

Say: **Not everyone is skilled in sports or in helping others. But each of us has a unique collection of abilities and talents given to us by God. Our job as Christians is to use those abilities to do God's work.**

Collect the "This Is Me" handouts to be used in the next lesson.

CLOSING
(up to 5 minutes)

OPTION 1: UNIQUE CREATION

Form pairs. Give kids each a piece of paper and some tape. Have them each tear, fold, tape or otherwise form the paper into a three-dimensional unique creation. Then have kids each present their creation to their partner while saying at least one thing they appreciate about that person's God-given abilities. Remind kids to be sincere because that's a great way to show God's love.

Form a circle and have kids each hold up their creation. Be specific and thank each person for an ability or talent he or she has. Encourage kids to keep their paper creations as reminders of God's creation of them as unique individuals.

OPTION 2: TALENTS

Have kids form a straight line. As you walk down the line and place your hand over each person's head, have the rest of the kids call out talents and abilities that person has. Be sensitive to kids who may not be well-liked by classmates and be sure to add your own comments for each person. Remind kids to be serious.

Close by having kids each say a one-sentence prayer, thanking God for one specific ability they have.

If You Still Have Time . . .

Who Am I?—Have kids play the Who Am I? game. Have each person think of someone living or dead. Then have them write three sentences that person might say that would describe him or her. Read the sentences aloud and have kids guess who they describe. Afterward, discuss how people become known for certain abilities or characteristics. Then have kids write three sentences that describe themselves. Collect the sentences and read them without revealing who wrote them. Have kids guess who wrote them.

Ability Cards—Give kids each a 3×5 card and a pencil. Have kids each sign their card and write on it one ability or talent they have that could be used to help someone in the class. For example, someone might write that he or she is good in math and could help tutor someone. Or someone might write he or she is good with kids and could babysit for a class member's siblings one day. Collect the cards. Then pass the cards around the room. Have kids each read the cards and silently decide how they might benefit from someone else's abilities.

UNIQUE PEOPLE

Find people who can honestly sign the following boxes. If the box describes an action, have them perform the action before signing the box. Return to the room at the designated time.

1. I love anchovies.

2. I've never seen "The Cosby Show."

3. ACTION: I can curl my tongue.

4. I put ketchup on my eggs.

5. ACTION: I can wiggle my ears.

6. I have never eaten a Twinkie.

7. ACTION: I can tap dance.

8. I drink milk out of the container.

9. I played in a rock 'n' roll band.

10. ACTION: I can say, "Pass the potatoes" in a foreign language.

11. I like peanut-butter-and-banana sandwiches.

12. I like liver and onions.

13. I can juggle.

14. ACTION: I can sing a song in German.

TAPPITY TAP TAP

VIASI, TAFADHALI * SWAHILI

KARTOFFELN, BITTE ! *

* GERMAN

THIS IS ME

Complete Section One, then fold your paper in half and have your partner complete Section Two of your handout. Talk about the completed handouts with your partner.

Section One

List five things you like to do.
1.
2.
3.
4.
5.

Write five words that describe you.
1.
2.
3.
4.
5.

List three things that really bother you about the world.
1.
2.
3.

Section Two

Complete the following sections about your partner. No peeking!
What five activities do you think your partner likes best?
1.
2.
3.
4.
5.

Write five words or phrases that describe your partner.
1.
2.
3.
4.
5.

List three things you think really bother your partner.
1.
2.
3.

LESSON 4

I CAN MAKE A DIFFERENCE

Once junior highers learn what their abilities are, they can learn to apply those abilities in doing God's work. And one way they can use their abilities is to help others.

LESSON AIM

To help build self-confidence in junior highers.

OBJECTIVES

Students will:
- experience serving others;
- reflect on how it feels to use their abilities to help others;
- discover how Abraham and Peter were changed when they discovered how God wanted them to use their abilities; and
- share their gifts with each other.

BIBLE BASIS
GENESIS 17:1-8
MATTHEW 16:13-19

Look up the following scriptures. Then read the background paragraphs to see how the passages relate to your junior highers or middle schoolers.

In **Genesis 17:1-8**, God makes a covenant with Abram and renames him Abraham.

When God changed Abram's name to Abraham, he established a new relationship with him. Abram means "exalted father," but Abraham means "father of many." This new name gave focus to Abraham's identity and his purpose as established by God.

Junior highers may have a hard time focusing on their identity if they don't see how their abilities fit in God's purpose. They need to realize that God has named them, too, and they can use their abilities for his purpose.

In **Matthew 16:13-19**, Simon confesses Christ and is renamed Peter by Jesus.

Simon's new name, Peter, helps us see his purpose as a disciple. Peter, which means "rock," was to be the foundation of the church. Through Jesus' insight and knowledge, he challenged Peter to use his abilities for purposes of the kingdom.

Junior highers can be challenged to use their abilities too. Just as Jesus helped Peter head in the right direction, he can help kids find their identity and purpose.

THIS LESSON AT A GLANCE

Section	Minutes	What Students Will Do	Supplies
Opener (Option 1)	5 to 10	**The Missing Piece**—Work together to complete puzzles.	Posters (cut into puzzle pieces), tape
(Option 2)		**Giving**—Discuss when it's easy and difficult to give to others.	Pencil, paper
Action and Reflection	10 to 15	**Caring Actions**—Experience using their abilities to care for others.	Newsprint, marker
Bible Application	10 to 15	**Changed Names**—Discuss how God helped Abraham and Peter see their abilities.	Bibles, newsprint, marker
Commitment	10 to 15	**What I Can Give**—Receive new names and determine how they can use their abilities to help others.	"This Is Me" handouts from Lesson 3, 3×5 cards, pencils, pins, "Gift List" handouts (p. 40)
Closing (Option 1)	up to 5	**The Gift Exchange**—Give people gifts in appreciation of their abilities.	Envelopes, pencils, magazines
(Option 2)		**Sharing Who I Am**—Tell why they're worthwhile.	

The Lesson

OPTION 1: THE MISSING PIECE

OPENER
(5 to 10 minutes)

Before the Lesson—Collect large posters of any design one for each group of five in your class. Cut each poster into 30- or 40-piece puzzles.

Form teams of no more than five. Give each team one poster puzzle and tape. Have team members divide the pieces evenly among themselves.

Then say: **We're going to start today's class with a contest. The first team to complete its puzzle will win. Only one team member may talk and a different team member must be in charge of taping the puzzle together. The rest of the team members may attempt to assemble the puzzle. You'll have only three minutes to put your puzzle together.**

Give teams a moment to decide who'll talk, tape and assemble the puzzle. On "go," have teams begin putting their puzzles together. After three minutes, call time. Declare the winning team.

Ask:

● **How did you feel as you tried to complete the puzzle?** (Frustrated; anxious; challenged.)

● **What different roles did people play in trying to complete the puzzle?** (Leader; follower; organizer; worker.)

● **How are these roles like the different abilities God's given each of us?** (Some people are good leaders; some people are good followers.)

Say: **Today we're going to tie up our course on self-esteem by challenging each other to discover how our unique abilities and gifts can help others.**

OPTION 2: GIVING

Write each person's name on a separate slip of paper. Fold the slips and place them on a table. Have kids each draw a name other than their own. Then have them each find an object in the room to give to that person as a gift of appreciation. Encourage kids to be creative. After they each "present" their gift, form a circle.

Ask:

● **How did you feel giving this gift?** (Embarrassed; stupid; uncomfortable; I enjoyed it.)

● **Was it easy to give this gift? Why or why not?** (Yes, I like giving gifts; no, I didn't know what I could give.)

● **When is it easy to give a gift to someone?** (When you know that person; when they deserve it; when they don't expect it.)

● **Which is easier—giving a gift or giving of yourself? Explain.** (A physical gift, giving of yourself is embarrassing; giving of yourself, it's easy for me to show I care about someone.)

Say: **Giving a gift can be a fun experience. But it can also be difficult—especially when you don't know what to give. Today we're going to see how each of us can give of ourselves.**

CARING ACTIONS

Have kids brainstorm caring actions they can carry out in class. For example, kids might suggest complimenting someone, offering a hug or helping someone find a scripture passage. Write kids' suggestions on a sheet of newsprint. Then have kids each choose one action they feel most comfortable with. On "go," have kids go around and perform that caring action for other people. If you have a small class, you might want to arrange ahead of time to have kids visit adult classes to perform the caring actions too. Then regroup and form a circle.

Ask:

● **How did you feel as you performed your caring actions?** (Good; uncomfortable.)

● **How did different caring actions use different abilities?** (Giving compliments required good speaking skills; helping someone find a scripture required good knowledge of the Bible; giving a hug required freedom to express emotion.)

● **What does this exercise show us about how we can use our unique abilities to help others?** (We don't all have to be great talkers or huggers; each person can offer something different.)

Have kids each complete the following sentence: "When I use my abilities to help someone else, I feel . . . "

Say: **God knows our strengths and weaknesses. And he knows how to help us use our strengths to the best of our ability, just as he helped Abraham and Peter.**

CHANGED NAMES

Form groups of no more than four. Have someone in each group read aloud Genesis 17:1-8 and Matthew 16:13-19. As kids read, write the following questions on newsprint for groups to discuss.

● What happened to the two men in these passages?

● Why were Abram and Simon given new names?

● What did each new name signify about that person's future?

● How would you feel if God gave you a new name that symbolized how you were to use your abilities?

After groups spend time discussing the questions, say: **Today our names identify us but rarely have any deeper meaning. In Bible times, names often reflected the person's mission or purpose in life. Peter means "rock." And Jesus said he would build his church on this "rock."**

WHAT I CAN GIVE

Form pairs. Return the "This Is Me" handouts from Lesson 3 to students to help them think about their abilities. Have partners brainstorm new names God might give them based on their abilities. Suggest kids think of positive words for

ACTION AND REFLECTION
(10 to 15 minutes)

BIBLE APPLICATION
(10 to 15 minutes)

COMMITMENT
(10 to 15 minutes)

their new names. Remind them to be serious during this activity. Then have kids each write their new name on a 3×5 card and pin it to their shirt.

Distribute a "Gift List" handout (p. 40) to each student. Have kids read over the list and find specific ways they can use their abilities. Have them each choose at least two items from the "Gift List" they can commit to working on in the coming week. Have them complete the commitment section at the bottom of the handout. Then have partners share practical ways they can help each other follow through with that commitment, such as phone calls or letters of encouragement.

Say: **Each of us has a great deal to offer. God has created each person in his image. Whether short or tall, smart or not-so-smart, each of us plays an important part in God's kingdom. Look at your "Gift Lists."** (Pause.) **Think about how you can use these God-given gifts to help others.**

CLOSING
(up to 5 minutes)

OPTION 1: THE GIFT EXCHANGE

Say: **As this course on boosting self-esteem comes to a close, think about all the unique talents and abilities represented in this room.**

Describe unique things about each student. For example, John is a good listener or Maria is a good discussion leader.

Say: **Now we'll each have a chance to share our uniqueness with others.**

Have kids each write their name on a different envelope. Place the envelopes around the room. Then have students look through magazines and tear out words or pictures that represent a gift they'd like to give each person in the room. Have them place these pictures or words in the appropriate envelopes. For example, someone might give a picture of a heart to symbolize the gift of caring or love. Remind kids to give sincere "gifts" to each person in the class. Collect the envelopes and seal them. Then give them to their owners.

Tell kids to take the envelopes home before opening them. Then encourage them to refer often to these "gifts" given by others to remind them of their own gifts and abilities.

Close in prayer, asking God to renew in each person a sense of self-worth based on God's love.

OPTION 2: SHARING WHO I AM

Form a circle. Have kids take turns affirming their gifts by completing the following sentence: "I am worthwhile because God gave me the gift of . . ." After each person has spoken, have students put their arms around each other to form a group hug. Close in prayer, thanking God for each class member specifically.

If You Still Have Time . . .

Course Reflection—Form a circle. Ask students to reflect on the past four sessions. Have them take turns completing the following sentences:

- Something I learned in this course was . . .
- If I could tell my friends about this course, I'd say . . .
- Something I'll do differently because of this course is . . .

Self-Esteem Partners—Have kids each choose a partner they know well. Have partners brainstorm ways they can boost each other's self-esteem during the coming week. Then have them commit to doing those things.

Use this list to help you connect your interests and abilities with specific gifts you may have. At the bottom of the page, list specific ways you can use these gifts to help friends and do God's work.

Based on your abilities and interests, which of the following gifts do you have? (Check each box that applies.)

Ways I can use my gifts to help others and do God's work:

_____

_____

_____

_____

_____

BONUS IDEAS

Self-Esteem Stoppers—Distribute 3×5 cards to junior highers. Have them each write "I feel good about myself when . . ." on one side of the card and "I don't feel good about myself when . . ." on the other. Then form groups of no more than four and have kids brainstorm ways to complete the sentences. Have them each write those ideas on their card. Encourage kids to keep their cards with them as reminders of what they can do to build a positive self-image.

High and Low Self-Esteem—Go to a shopping mall or airport with your junior highers. Have kids sit and watch the people who walk by. Have them take notes describing people they think might have high self-esteem and people they think might have low self-esteem. Then talk about how self-esteem affects the way people dress, look or act.

Adopt a Friend—Have students each choose a school acquaintance they feel has low self-esteem and secretly "adopt" him or her. Have kids each think up creative ways to help that person feel good about him- or herself. For example, kids might call this person, sit with him or her at lunch, or leave notes of encouragement in his or her locker. Have regular follow-up sessions with your junior highers to see how the adoption program is going.

Servant Session—Meet with junior highers for a "servant session" where kids can help others. Choose projects where kids can see a difference because of what they do; for example: painting a house, raking leaves, fixing up a run-down house or cleaning up a neighborhood alley. Then talk with kids about how they felt as they helped others. Talk with junior highers about how helping others affects their self-esteem.

Esteem-Booster Club—Have your kids form an Esteem-Booster Club. Help them brainstorm practical ways to help kids feel better about themselves. Then create a hotline kids can call when they know of someone in the group who feels down. Use this hotline to prompt club members to do something special for kids who're feeling bad about themselves. Have the Esteem-Booster Club sponsor parties where kids can have fun without the fear of being put down.

Expectation Bingo—Make a copy of the "Expectation Bingo" handout (p. 44) and cut apart the squares. Fold these and place them in a box. Then give junior highers each a copy of

MEETINGS AND MORE

BONUS SCRIPTURES

The lessons focus on a select few scripture passages, but if you'd like to incorporate more Bible readings into the lessons, here are our suggestions:
- 1 Samuel 16:1-13 (God chooses David to be king.)
- Jeremiah 1:4-10 (God calls Jeremiah to be a prophet.)
- Luke 19:1-10 (Jesus visits Zacchaeus.)
- 1 Corinthians 12:1-11 (Paul describes the variety of spiritual gifts.)
- Psalm 139:1-16 (God created each person in an amazing and wonderful way.)

the "Expectation Bingo" handout and a pencil. Draw a square out of the box and read it. Have kids mark that word with an "X" if they feel confident about themselves in that area or an "O" if they feel insecure in that area. Ask them to call out "Bingo" if they get four X's or O's in a row. After the game, form pairs and have kids discuss their handouts and talk about expectations.

Ask:
● **What danger is there if we expect too much of ourselves?**
● **How do our own expectations affect our self-esteem?**

Table Talk—Use the "Table Talk" handout (p. 25) as the basis for a parents and junior higher's meeting. Prepare fun, nonthreatening crowdbreakers for kids and their parents to do together. Be sure to include times for parents and kids to affirm each other. For crowdbreaker ideas, check out *Quick Crowdbreakers and Games for Youth Groups* (Group Books).

Plan a variety of discussion groups: kids only, parents only, and kids and parents together. Have groups discuss the importance of healthy self-esteem and how that differs from overconfidence or boasting.

Close with a meaningful time of worship where kids and parents give thanks for their God-given gifts.

RETREAT IDEAS

Unique Retreat—Celebrate differences with junior highers. Encourage kids to wear clothes that reflect who they are. Encourage them to bring games, books or music they like. Then have an opening meeting where kids can each share unique things about themselves with the rest of the group. For example, one junior higher might give everyone else a cookie because he or she likes to bake. Another might play his or her favorite song. Allot a specific time limit for junior highers to express themselves.

If possible, hold the retreat in a unique place, such as a barn, warehouse, office building or garage.

Focus on the positive aspects of each person's uniqueness.

Carry Caring Retreat—Spend a weekend carrying caring within and beyond your group. Begin the retreat with an evening of exercises that help kids care for each other, such as back rubs or sandwich-making. The next day, have kids take their caring attitudes to various projects, such as washing windows, cleaning houses or raking leaves for elderly church members. Reconvene at night to talk about the day and how people feel about their caring activities. Close the weekend with a creative worship where kids show how they care for each other without speaking.

Family Affirmations—Have your kids sponsor a family affirmation night. Help junior highers plan fun games, discussion times and refreshments. Remind kids to make the evening a time of fun, uplifting activities. Then invite entire families to attend.

"I Am Who I Am" Party—Have kids attend a party wearing clothes that best represent who they are. Tell them they can wear strange, wacky clothes or dress up in suits and fancy dresses if they like. Encourage each person to be creative. At the party, have kids play games, eat and participate in discussions in any way they like.

After the party, discuss how easy or difficult it is to be yourself at school or with friends. Have kids commit to seek new ways to express their true identity instead of just meeting others' expectations.

PARTY PLEASERS

EXPECTATION BINGO

Schoolwork	Making money	Future	Speaking ability
Friends	Intelligence	Parents	Athletic ability
Looks	Grades	Dealing with brother/sister	Musical ability
Clothes	Church activities	Body shape	Dating

CURRICULUM REORDER—TOP PRIORITY

Order now to prepare for your upcoming Sunday school classes, youth ministry meetings, and weekend retreats! Each book includes all teacher and student materials—plus photocopiable handouts—for any size class . . . for just $8.99 each!

FOR SENIOR HIGH:

1 & 2 Corinthians: Christian Discipleship, ISBN 1-55945-230-7

Angels, Demons, Miracles & Prayer, ISBN 1-55945-235-8

Changing the World, ISBN 1-55945-236-6

Christians in a Non-Christian World, ISBN 1-55945-224-2

Christlike Leadership, ISBN 1-55945-231-5

Communicating With Friends, ISBN 1-55945-228-5

Counterfeit Religions, ISBN 1-55945-207-2

Dating Decisions, ISBN 1-55945-215-3

Dealing With Life's Pressures, ISBN 1-55945-232-3

Deciphering Jesus' Parables, ISBN 1-55945-237-4

Exodus: Following God, ISBN 1-55945-226-9

Exploring Ethical Issues, ISBN 1-55945-225-0

Faith for Tough Times, ISBN 1-55945-216-1

Forgiveness, ISBN 1-55945-223-4

Getting Along With Parents, ISBN 1-55945-202-1

Getting Along With Your Family, ISBN 1-55945-233-1

The Gospel of John: Jesus' Teachings, ISBN 1-55945-208-0

Hazardous to Your Health: AIDS, Steroids & Eating Disorders, ISBN 1-55945-200-5

Is Marriage in Your Future?, ISBN 1-55945-203-X

Jesus' Death & Resurrection, ISBN 1-55945-211-0

The Joy of Serving, ISBN 1-55945-210-2

Knowing God's Will, ISBN 1-55945-205-6

Life After High School, ISBN 1-55945-220-X

Making Good Decisions, ISBN 1-55945-209-9

Money: A Christian Perspective, ISBN 1-55945-212-9

Movies, Music, TV & Me, ISBN 1-55945-213-7

Overcoming Insecurities, ISBN 1-55945-221-8

Psalms, ISBN 1-55945-234-X

Real People, Real Faith: Amy Grant, Joni Eareckson Tada, Dave Dravecky, Terry Anderson, ISBN 1-55945-238-2

Responding to Injustice, ISBN 1-55945-214-5

Revelation, ISBN 1-55945-229-3

School Struggles, ISBN 1-55945-201-3

Sex: A Christian Perspective, ISBN 1-55945-206-4

Today's Lessons From Yesterday's Prophets, ISBN 1-55945-227-7

Turning Depression Upside Down, ISBN 1-55945-135-1

What Is the Church?, ISBN 1-55945-222-6

Who Is God?, ISBN 1-55945-218-8

Who Is Jesus?, ISBN 1-55945-219-6

Who Is the Holy Spirit?, ISBN 1-55945-217-X

Your Life as a Disciple, ISBN 1-55945-204-8

FOR JUNIOR HIGH/MIDDLE SCHOOL:

Accepting Others: Beyond Barriers & Stereotypes, ISBN 1-55945-126-2

Advice to Young Christians: Exploring Paul's Letters, ISBN 1-55945-146-7

Applying the Bible to Life, ISBN 1-55945-116-5

Becoming Responsible, ISBN 1-55945-109-2

Bible Heroes: Joseph, Esther, Mary & Peter, ISBN 1-55945-137-8

Boosting Self-Esteem, ISBN 1-55945-100-9

Building Better Friendships, ISBN 1-55945-138-6

Can Christians Have Fun?, ISBN 1-55945-134-3

Caring for God's Creation, ISBN 1-55945-121-1

Christmas: A Fresh Look, ISBN 1-55945-124-6

Competition, ISBN 1-55945-133-5

Dealing With Death, ISBN 1-55945-112-2

Dealing With Disappointment, ISBN 1-55945-139-4

Doing Your Best, ISBN 1-55945-142-4

Drugs & Drinking, ISBN 1-55945-118-1

Evil and the Occult, ISBN 1-55945-102-5

Genesis: The Beginnings, ISBN 1-55945-111-4

Guys & Girls: Understanding Each Other, ISBN 1-55945-110-6

Handling Conflict, ISBN 1-55945-125-4

Heaven & Hell, ISBN 1-55945-131-9

Is God Unfair?, ISBN 1-55945-108-4

Love or Infatuation?, ISBN 1-55945-128-9

Making Parents Proud, ISBN 1-55945-107-6

Making the Most of School, ISBN 1-55945-113-0

Materialism, ISBN 1-55945-130-0

The Miracle of Easter, ISBN 1-55945-143-2

Miracles!, ISBN 1-55945-117-3

Peace & War, ISBN 1-55945-123-8

Peer Pressure, ISBN 1-55945-103-3

Prayer, ISBN 1-55945-104-1

Reaching Out to a Hurting World, ISBN 1-55945-140-8

Sermon on the Mount, ISBN 1-55945-129-7

Suicide: The Silent Epidemic, ISBN 1-55945-145-9

Telling Your Friends About Christ, ISBN 1-55945-114-9

The Ten Commandments, ISBN 1-55945-127-0

Today's Faith Heroes: Madeline Manning Mims, Michael W. Smith, Mother Teresa, Bruce Olson, ISBN 1-55945-141-6

Today's Media: Choosing Wisely, ISBN 1-55945-144-0

Today's Music: Good or Bad?, ISBN 1-55945-101-7

What Is God's Purpose for Me?, ISBN 1-55945-132-7

What's a Christian?, ISBN 1-55945-105-X

Order today from your local Christian bookstore, or write: Group Publishing, Box 485, Loveland, CO 80539. For mail orders, please add postage/handling of $4 for orders up to $15, $5 for orders of $15.01+. Colorado residents add 3% sales tax.

MORE PROGRAMMING IDEAS FOR YOUR ACTIVE GROUP...

DO IT! ACTIVE LEARNING IN YOUTH MINISTRY

Thom and Joani Schultz

Discover the keys to teaching creative faith-building lessons that teenagers look forward to...and remember for a lifetime. You'll learn how to design simple, fun programs that will help your kids...

- build community,

- develop communication skills,

- relate better to others,

- experience what it's really like to be a Christian,

...and apply the Bible to their daily challenges. Plus, you'll get 24 ready-to-use active-learning exercises complete with debriefing questions and Bible application. For example, your kids will...

- learn the importance of teamwork and the value of each team member by juggling six different objects as a group,

- experience community and God's grace using a doughnut,

- grow more sensitive to others' needs by acting out Matthew 25:31-46

...just to name a few. And the practical index of over 30 active-learning resources will make your planning easier.

ISBN 0-931529-94-8

DEVOTIONS FOR YOUTH GROUPS ON THE GO

Dan and Cindy Hansen

Now it's easy to turn every youth group trip into an opportunity for spiritual growth for your kids. This resource gives you 52 easy-to-prepare devotions that teach meaningful spiritual lessons using the experiences of your group's favorite outings. You'll get devotions perfect for everything from amusement parks, to choir trips, to miniature golf, to the zoo. Your kids will gain new insights from the Bible as they...

- discuss how many "strikes" God gives us—after enjoying a game of softball,

- experience the hardship of Jesus' temptation in the wilderness—on a camping trip,

- understand the disciples' relief when Jesus calmed the storm—while white-water rafting, even

...learn to trust God's will when bad weather cancels an event or the bus breaks down!

Plus, the handy topical listing makes your planning easy.

ISBN 1-55945-075-4

Order today from your local Christian bookstore, or write: Group Publishing, Box 485, Loveland, CO 80539. For mail orders, please add postage/handling of $4 for orders up to $15, $5 for orders of $15.01+. Colorado residents add 3% sales tax.